ANIMAL ATTACK

KILLER CATS

Alex Woolf

ARCTURUS

This edition first published in 2011 by Arcturus Publishing

Distributed by Black Rabbit Books
P.O. Box 3263
Mankato
Minnesota MN 56002

Copyright © 2011 Arcturus Publishing Limited

Printed in China

Library of Congress Cataloging-in-Publication Data

Woolf, Alex, 1964-
 Killer cats / Alex Woolf.
    p. cm. -- (Animal attack)
 Includes index.
 ISBN 978-1-84837-946-6 (library binding)
 1. Panthera--Juvenile literature. 2. Predatory animals--Juvenile literature. 3. Dangerous animals--Juvenile
literature. I. Title.
 QL737.C23W68 2012
 599.75'5--dc22

                          2011006626

The right of Alex Woolf to be identified as the author of this work has been asserted by him in accordance with the
Copyright, Designs and Patents Act 1988.

Series concept: Alex Woolf
Editor and picture researcher: Alex Woolf
Designer: Ian Winton
Cover designer: Peter Ridley

Picture credits
Nature Picture Library: 7 (Anup Shah), 12 (Andy Rouse), 13 (Anup Shah), 16 (Anup Shah),
17 (Anup Shah), 19 top (Luiz Claudio Marigo), 20 (Nick Gordon), 25 (Anup Shah), 27 (Eric Baccega),
29 (Lynn M. Stone).
Shutterstock: cover (Cheryl Ann Quigley), 4 (Eric Isselée), 5 top (Dennis Donohue), 5 bottom (Tiago
Jorge da Silva Estima), 6 (Nagel Photography), 8 (Peter Blackwell), 9 (Uryadnikov Sergey), 10 (neelsky),
11 (hxdbzxy), 14 (Eric Isselée), 15 (EcoPrint), 18 (Karen Givens), 19 bottom (Ewan Chesser), 21 (Dean
Bertoncelj), 22 (creativex), 23 (Tony Rix), 24 (Eric Gevaert), 28 (Volodymyr Burdiak).
Tambako The Jaguar: 26.

Supplier 03, Date 0411, Print Run 1042
SL001707US

Contents

Big Beasts

The cats we see every day in our homes and streets make charming and gentle pets. They aren't scary at all—unless you happen to be a mouse! But their bigger cousins are truly ferocious predators.

Lions have a noble appearance and are sometimes called "kings of the jungle." They actually live in the African savannah.

All big cats are carnivores—they eat only meat. They are found in the Americas, Africa, Asia, and Europe, from cold mountaintops to the sweltering savannah.

SNACK ON THIS!

Big cats are famous for their roar. When they breathe out, the walls of the cat's larynx (voice box) vibrate, producing a deep, loud, rumbling sound. Lions have the longest larynx, giving them the most powerful roar.

Big cats are superb hunter-killers. They have keen eyesight, including night vision, and highly sensitive hearing. Their speed in the chase, sharp teeth and claws, and powerful jaws give them huge advantages when hunting for prey.

Most big cats, like their smaller relatives, can climb trees. This is a cougar, or mountain lion.

Big cat facts

- **Prey:** Antelope, warthog, buffalo, hare, monkey, wildebeest, zebra, gazelle, deer, boar
- **Tools:** Eyesight, hearing, strength, speed, agility, sharp teeth and claws
- **Methods:** Concealment through camouflage, search and stalk, chase, ambush, killing bite to the throat

Tigers are the largest of the big cats and are found in Asia.

Lions

The lion is a large, powerful predator that lives in the grasslands of sub-Saharan Africa and Asia. Among the big cats, it is second only in size to the tiger.

Male lions are famous for their manes. In clashes with other animals, the mane makes the lion look bigger.

SNACK ON THIS!

The heaviest lion ever recorded was a male called Simba living at Colchester Zoo in the UK. It weighed 825 lb. when it died in 1973.

Unlike most big cats, which tend to be solitary, lions live in groups called prides. There can be up to 40 lions in a pride, most of which are females. Together, prides defend a territory that can be as large as 200 square miles.

When it reaches maturity, a male lion will leave its original pride. It will fight the male of another pride to try and take its place. Older or injured male lions are vulnerable to attack by younger incoming males.

An adult male lion fights a younger male. Incoming males often kill the cubs of those they have driven out, to give their own, future offspring a better chance of survival.

Lion facts

- **Length:** Males can grow up to 10 ft.
- **Weight:** Males 330-400 lb.; females 260-400 lb.
- **Lifespan:** 10-14 years in the wild; 20 or more years in captivity

How Lions Hunt

Most of the hunting is done by female lions, or lionesses. They can run very fast, but only in short bursts.

A lioness chases a warthog. Lionesses can reach speeds of more than 50 miles per hour.

SNACK ON THIS!

Lions do most of their hunting at night. Their eyes are six times more sensitive to light than human eyes, so they can see very well in the dark.

The lionesses hunt as a team, splitting into two groups. The larger group chases the prey—usually a herd of grazing animals—towards a smaller group lying in wait. When the herd are no more than 100 feet away, the smaller group chase down their selected victim.

The attack is swift and brutal. They leap onto the prey and sink their claws into its hindquarters, bringing it down, and then deliver a killer bite to its head or neck.

Lions typically prey on zebra, wildebeest, and gazelle, although they sometimes hunt buffalo, hippo, and giraffe. Occasionally, lone male lions have been known to hunt humans. This usually happens because they are too injured or sick to hunt their usual prey.

CHEW ON THAT!

A man-eating lion in southern Tanzania killed and ate at least 35 people before it was shot in April 2004.

A lioness with her latest victim, a young antelope. After a hunt, the males are the first to eat, followed by the females, and finally the cubs.

9

Tigers

The tiger is the biggest of the big cats. There are five subspecies. The biggest, the Siberian, can reach a total length of 11 feet, while the smallest, the Sumatran, averages just 6 feet.

Tigers are among the most recognizable of the big cats. Their reddish orange fur and dark stripes provide ideal camouflage in the dense tropical forests of eastern and southern Asia where they live.

SNACK ON THIS!

The pattern of stripes is unique to each tiger, like fingerprints on humans. If you were to shave a tiger, you would find the same striped pattern on its skin.

The Royal Bengal tiger is the most numerous of all the tiger species and is the 'national animal' of Bangladesh.

Two tigers play fight in the water.

Unlike the lion, the tiger is a solitary beast, living and hunting alone. It defends its own territory aggressively against other tigers. A tiger's territory can range from 7 to 35 square miles, depending on how much prey there is.

Tigers are unusual among big cats in their love of water, and they can often be seen cooling off in ponds, lakes, and rivers. They have been known to swim more than 3 miles in a day.

Tiger facts

- **Length:** Males 6.5-11 ft.; females 6-8.5 ft. (depending on subspecies)

- **Weight:** Males 220–500 lb.; females 165-360 lb. (depending on subspecies)

- **Speed:** 30-40 mph in short bursts

How Tigers Hunt

Tigers hunt mainly at night. They target larger animals, such as wild boar, buffalo, and deer, but will hunt smaller animals such as monkeys, peafowl, hares, and fish when their favorites aren't available.

The tiger hunts alone, but has been known to share its kills with others in its family group. It ambushes its prey by hiding in thick vegetation and then leaping out when its victim strays near.

A tiger stalks a deer. It tries to get as close as possible to its prey before making the final charge.

SNACK ON THIS!

A tiger can cover up to 33 feet in a single leap.

The tiger grabs its prey with its forelimbs, using its size and strength to push the prey off balance. It then delivers a killing bite to the throat. It keeps its jaws clamped to the throat until the victim dies of suffocation.

Because of its use of strength, speed, and surprise, the tiger is able to overpower prey much larger than itself, including the water buffalo, which can weigh over a ton—six times heavier than its attacker.

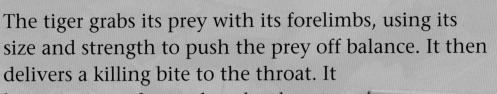

CHEW ON THAT!

Tigers have to be very patient: only one in twenty hunts ends in a kill.

A female tiger drags away her prey—a chital.

Leopards

The leopard is larger and stronger than the cheetah, but smaller and more lightly built than the jaguar.

Leopards are smaller than lions and tigers, with relatively short legs and a long body. Like jaguars (see pages 18–21), their fur is covered in rosettes, but leopard rosettes are smaller than jaguar ones, and have no internal spots.

The most adaptable of the big cats, leopards are found in desert, open grassland, forest, and mountain regions. The color of their fur varies from cream to deep gold, depending on where they live, to give them the best chance of blending into their surroundings.

SNACK ON THIS!

Some forest leopards are born with black fur and are known as panthers. Black-furred jaguars are also called panthers.

Leopards are solitary creatures, who are generally active at night. They spend their days resting on tree branches or in caves. Their powerful shoulder muscles make them excellent tree climbers. They are also good swimmers.

Sometimes they clash with other leopards when defending their territories, which can range from 6 to 30 square miles in size.

Leopards' tree climbing skills can come in handy when they face a threat from larger relatives such as lions and tigers.

Leopard facts

- **Length:** 6-8.5 ft.
- **Weight:** Male 65-200 lb.; female 50-130 lb.
- **Range:** Sub-Saharan Africa and Southeast Asia

How Leopards Hunt

Leopards are agile, stealthy predators, stalking their prey silently before pouncing with lethal suddenness. They clamp their powerful jaws around their victim's throat, holding on until the animal dies of suffocation.

A leopard stalks its prey.

SNACK ON THIS!

Leopards are the only big cats to hide their prey in trees. They can drag prey three times their own weight (including full-grown antelopes or even young giraffes) high into treetops.

In savannah and desert areas, leopards mostly hunt at night, while forest leopards often hunt during the day, using their natural camouflage to conceal themselves in the dense vegetation.

CHEW ON THAT!

In India, during the early 20th century, the so-called "Panar Leopard" turned man-eater after it was injured by a poacher and could no longer hunt its normal prey. It was believed to have killed around 400 people before being shot by a hunter.

A leopard grips an impala by the throat in a suffocation bite.

Leopards are not fussy eaters. They will eat virtually any animal they can catch, including insects, rodents, reptiles, and fish. However, they mainly target smaller antelope and deer, such as impalas, gazelles, chitals, and duikers.

Leopards living near human settlements have been known to attack domestic livestock such as goats and pigs, and occasionally even people.

Jaguars

The jaguar is the largest big cat in the Western Hemisphere and the third largest overall. It inhabits the forests and grassy plains of Central and South America.

Like tigers, jaguars love swimming and are often found near water. They are also good tree climbers. Once mature, jaguars spend much of their lives alone, meeting only to mate. Their most active times are during the hours of dawn and dusk.

The jaguar looks similar to the leopard, but it is larger and more powerfully built, with a rounder head. Its rosettes are also bigger than the leopard's and have small spots in the middle.

SNACK ON THIS!

The jaguar's roar sounds similar to a repeated cough. It is also known to make grunting and mewing sounds.

Jaguar facts

- **Length:** 7.8–8.5 ft.
- **Weight:** Male 200–250 lb.; female 130–200 lb.
- **Range:** Mexico in the north to Paraguay and northern Argentina in the south

(Above) Jaguars generally avoid each other, but sometimes they clash over disputed territory. Male territories range from 15 to 25 square miles. Female territories are roughly half that.

Like leopards, jaguars are sometimes born with black fur and are known as panthers. Although they appear perfectly black, their spots are visible on close inspection.

How Jaguars Hunt

The jaguar hunts alone, stalking and ambushing its prey. It prefers the larger mammals and reptiles of the forest and the grassland plains, such as deer, tapirs, capybaras, and caimans, but will make do with foxes, frogs, and rodents. It may also hunt monkeys and sloths in the lower branches of trees.

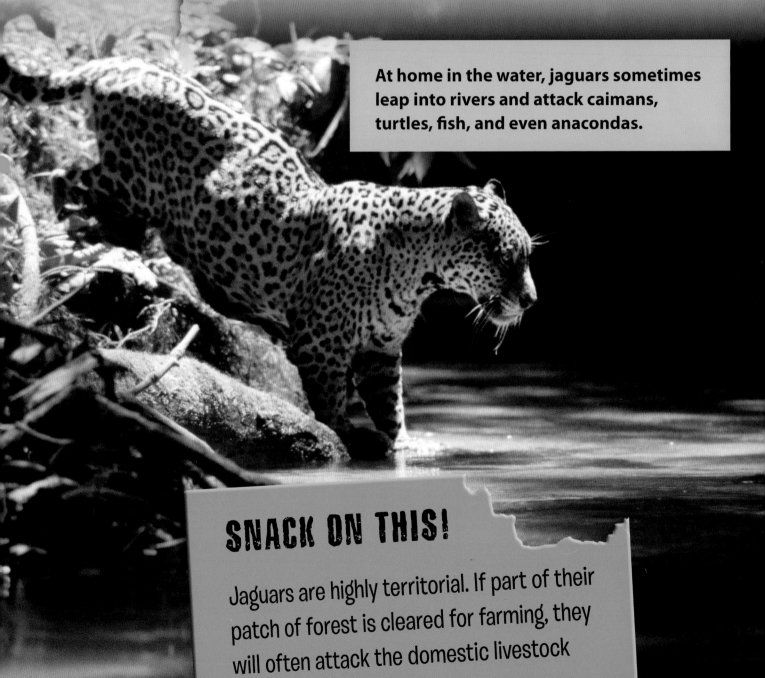

At home in the water, jaguars sometimes leap into rivers and attack caimans, turtles, fish, and even anacondas.

SNACK ON THIS!

Jaguars are highly territorial. If part of their patch of forest is cleared for farming, they will often attack the domestic livestock they find grazing there.

Walking slowly down forest paths, the jaguar listens for its prey. When the target is sighted, it creeps closer, finding a concealed position to the rear of the animal, before pouncing. It kills its prey with a powerful bite to the skull between the ears, piercing the brain.

Its muscular jaws and long, sharp canines allow the jaguar to bite through the shells of turtles or armored reptiles.

CHEW ON THAT!

The jaguar has the strongest bite of all the big cats. In fact the only mammal with a stronger bite is the spotted hyena. The jaguar can bite down with over a ton of force—twice the bite strength of a lion.

Cougars

The cougar is found right across the Western Hemisphere, from Canada to Chile. An extremely adaptable animal, it thrives in a range of habitats, including mountains, forests, prairies, and deserts.

Perhaps because of this, the cougar has a remarkable number of names, known in different places as puma, mountain lion, red tiger, deercat, mountain devil, Mexican lion, mountain screamer, catamount, and sneak cat.

Cougars are lean, agile creatures with round heads and erect ears. They are the only big cat without fur markings, apart from the African lion.

SNACK ON THIS!

Unlike other big cats, the cougar cannot roar, but it can make other surprising sounds, such as chirps, peeps, whistles, and even screams.

Its strong hind limbs allow the cougar to make giant leaps of up to 20 feet in pursuit of prey.

The cougar is a stalk-and-ambush predator, armed with long, sharp canines and retractable claws. It can kill an elk by jumping on its back and pulling with its forelegs to break its neck. It will often bury its kill to conceal it from scavengers.

Cougar facts

- **Length:** Male average 8 ft.; female average 6.6 ft.

- **Weight:** Male 115-200 lb.; female 65-140 lb.

- **Prey:** Anything from mouse to moose; it prefers larger animals such as deer and elk, but will eat insects, rabbits, raccoons, bats, frogs, and rodents

Cheetahs

The cheetah is built for one purpose: speed. It lives in the flat, treeless, grassy plains of sub-Saharan Africa where swiftness in the chase is a huge advantage for a predator.

It is helped by a streamlined body, strong, thin legs and light bones. It also boasts hard-padded paws and semiretractable claws for grip, and large nostrils and lungs for extra oxygen in the closing stages of a sprint.

The cheetah can easily be identified by the black rings on its tail and the "tear marks" on its face.

SNACK ON THIS!

The cheetah has a top speed of 71 mph, making it the world's fastest land animal.

The cheetah has very good eyesight, so prefers to hunt during the day. It follows herds of gazelle or impala, looking for old, young or injured animals. Once it has found its target, it will creep to within 150 feet before giving chase. Full sprints last around 20 seconds.

The cheetah's flexible spine works like a spring for its back legs, giving it extra reach for each stride.

With its exceptional speed, the cheetah usually manages to outrun its victims. After bringing down the animal, the cheetah clamps its powerful jaws around its windpipe, suffocating it.

Cheetah facts

- **Length:** 6.1-7 ft.
- **Weight:** 80-140 lb.
- **Markings:** Yellow or tan fur with solid black round or oval spots

Snow Leopards

The snow leopard is a solitary cat inhabiting the mountains of Central Asia. Its thick, woolly fur keeps it warm in its chilly environment. The fur is white, yellowish or smoky grey and covered in dark gray rosettes, providing it with excellent camouflage on rocky mountainsides.

Snow leopards are shy, elusive cats, rarely seen in the wild.

SNACK ON THIS!

The snow leopard's powerful hind legs enable it to leap over 30 feet–five times its body length.

The cat's short forelimbs and long hind legs give it agility on steep, rugged mountain slopes. Its tail gives it balance, and its large paws help it to walk on snow. All these attributes help it when hunting mountain sheep and goats—its favored prey.

The snow leopard hunts at dawn and dusk. It kills large animals roughly twice a month. These can take several days to devour.

A mother snow leopard with her cub. Snow leopards spend most of their lives alone, and when this cub matures, at the age of 18 to 22 months, it will move far away, seeking new hunting grounds.

Snow leopard facts

- **Length:** 6-7.5 ft.
- **Weight:** 75-120 lb.
- **Sounds:** Mewing, hissing, growling, moaning, and yowling (it cannot roar)

When sheep or goats aren't available, the snow leopard will eat smaller animals such as marmots, hares, rodents, and birds. Unusually for a big cat, it will sometimes even eat plants.

Lynxes

The lynx inhabits the remote forests and snowy wastes of northern Europe, Asia, and North America. It has soft, thick fur to keep it warm during the harsh winters and big feet to help it walk through deep snow.

A skilled climber, the lynx likes to spend much of its time in the branches of trees, waiting for prey such as mammals or non-flying birds to pass beneath it.

The tufts of black hair on the lynx's ears act as a hearing aid.

SNACK ON THIS!

A 33-lb. lynx has bigger feet than a 200-lb. cougar.

The favourite prey of the Canadian lynx is the snowshoe hare. So dependent is it on this prey that when snowshoe hare numbers decline, about once every ten years, there is a corresponding fall in the lynx population.

The lynx hunts by stalking and ambushing its prey. It has acute hearing and vision, sensitive whiskers and quick reflexes to help it hunt, both by day and night.

The lynx's eyesight is so good, it can spot a mouse 250 feet away. It also has enough strength and agility to catch and kill a reindeer or caribou, despite being no bigger than an average-sized dog.

Lynx facts

- **Length:** 3-4 ft.
- **Weight:** 20-45 lb.
- **Prey:** Snowshoe hares, deer, birds, sheep, goats, rodents, fish

Glossary

adaptable Able to adjust to different conditions.

agile Able to move quickly and easily.

ambush Launch a surprise attack from a concealed position.

anaconda A snake of the boa family that inhabits the swamps and rivers of tropical South America.

attribute A quality or feature of something.

caiman A member of the alligator family native to South America.

camouflage An animal's natural coloring or form that enables it to blend in with its surroundings.

canines Pointed teeth used by meat-eating mammals for piercing skin and tearing and ripping flesh.

capybara A South American rodent that looks like a giant, long-legged guinea pig.

carcass The dead body of an animal.

caribou A large North American reindeer.

chital A deer native to India and Sri Lanka.

domestic livestock Tame animals, kept by farmers.

duiker A small African antelope.

elk A large North American red deer.

elusive Difficult to find.

habitat A creature's natural environment.

impala A type of antelope of southern and East Africa.

marmot A heavily built, burrowing rodent of Eurasia and North America.

moose A large deer native to northern Eurasia and North America.

poacher A person who hunts illegally.

retractable claws Claws that can be pulled back inside an animal's body.

rosette A rose-shaped marking.

savannah A grassy plain in tropical or subtropical regions.

scavenger Animal that eats carrion or other discarded food.

sloth A slow-moving, tropical American mammal.

species A group of animals that are similar enough to interbreed.

stalk Pursue or approach stealthily.

stealthy Moving quietly and cautiously.

sub-Saharan Africa The part of Africa south of the Sahara desert.

subspecies One of a number of distinct groups of animals all belonging to a single species, but usually geographically isolated from each other.

suffocation Death from lack of air.

tapir A hoofed mammal with a long, flexible snout, native to tropical America and Malaysia.

territorial Defending a territory or area.

tropical Of the tropics—the warmest region of the Earth, close to the equator.

warthog An African wild pig.

Western Hemisphere The half of the Earth that contains the Americas.

Further information

Books

Big Cats by Jonathan Sheikh-Miller, Stephanie Turnbull and John Woodcock (Usborne, 2010)

Big Cats by Monica Halpern (Rourke Books, 2010)

Big Cats by Steve Parker and Ian Jackson (Windmill Books, 2010)

Discover Animals: Discover Big Cats by Monalisa Sengupta (Enslow Publishers, 2008)

National Geographic Kids Everything Big Cats: Pictures to Purr About and Info to Make You Roar by Elizabeth Carney (National Geographic, 2011)

Web Sites

animals.nationalgeographic.com/animals/big-cats
   Videos of big cats in the wild.

www.bbc.co.uk/bigcat/index.shtml
   A BBC website devoted to the big cats of the Masai Mara game reserve
   in Kenya.

www.bigcats.com/learn-to-identify-the-big-cats
   Helps identify the different big cat species with the help of some
   great photos.

www.wildcatconservation.org
   Canadian site drawing attention to the threats facing cougars, lynxes, and
   other big cats and how people can help.

dialspace.dial.pipex.com/agarman/bco/ver4.htm
   A huge repository of information on big cats, with sections on each
   species.

Index

Page numbers in **bold** refer to pictures.